HITLER'S RISE TO POWER:

COULD IT HAVE BEEN PREVENTED?

TAYLOR SAPP

Alphabet Publishing

www.AlphabetPublish.com

Auschwitz Concentration Camp

Adolph Hitler, 1937

Map of proposed German expansion from *Mein Kampf*

Adolf Hitler's difficult early life, growing extreme beliefs, and anger over Germany's loss in World War I set the stage for his rise to power. His skill at taking advantage of problems and promising to make the country strong again led to his leadership of Nazi Germany, with tragic effects around the world. But what if Hitler had never risen to power?

INTRODUCTION

Adolf Hitler (1889–1945) was a leader from Austria who became the dictator of Germany. He led the Nazi Party and ruled from 1933 to 1945. Hitler believed in German or ethnic nationalism, creating a country where only certain people he called "pure" could live.

Hitler pushed a message of anti-Semitism, discrimination and persecution of Jewish people. This sadly led to the killing of six million Jewish people and millions of others during the Holocaust. He also started World War II in 1939 by invading other countries, causing terrible destruction.

Known for his powerful speeches, he gained control during a time when Germany was struggling after World War I. His rule ended when he lost the war and died in 1945.

Introductory Questions

1. Adolf Hitler is considered one of the most, if not the most, dangerous and evil leaders in world history. Why does Hitler have such a terrible image?

2. Read the infamous quote reported in 1943 by Walter C. Langer for the United States Office of Strategic Services in describing Hitler's psychological profile:

   "People will believe a big lie sooner than a little one; and if you repeat it frequently enough people will sooner or later believe it."

   - What does this quote mean?
   - Do you agree or disagree with this statement? Why?

3. What else do you know about Hitler? Can you think of anything important he did?

4. What do you know about other leaders with an image similar to Hitler?

5. What do you know about World War II?
   - What countries fought in the war and for which side?
   - What were the causes of the war?
   - How did it end?

CONTENTS

THE RISE AND FALL OF HITLER

Adolf Hitler was born in Austria on April 20, 1889. Adolf Hitler was born to Alois Hitler, a strict customs official, and Klara Pölzl, a nurturing mother. Frequent moves and his father's authoritarian parenting style left a lasting impact on young Adolf. Several of his brothers and sisters died as infants, fostering a sense of loneliness.

As a child, he had a strong interest in art and dreamed of becoming an artist. In 1907, he left his hometown of Linz to move to Vienna where he planned to study fine art. His mother supported him financially, but she passed away from breast cancer later that year, leaving Hitler without her help. He struggled to succeed in his art career, being rejected twice by the Academy of Fine Arts in Vienna. Without much money, he was sometimes homeless. He had to live on the streets, working small jobs and selling watercolor paintings of Vienna's buildings and streets.

Alois Hitler, ~1898

Adolph Hitler, ~1890

Klara Hitler, ~1875

While living in Vienna, Hitler became interested in other subjects like architecture and music. But his time there also exposed him to racist ideas, intense ethnic nationalism, anti-Semitism, and social Darwinism. He read newspapers and writings by anti-Semitic leaders like Karl Lueger and Georg Ritter von Schönerer. Lueger, Vienna's mayor, combined populist rhetoric with anti-Semitic policies. These writings spread hateful views against Jewish people and encouraged fear of Eastern European Jews. These ideologies profoundly influenced his worldview and they later became part of his political beliefs.

In 1913, Hitler moved to Germany and joined the German Army when World War I broke out in 1914. He served as a soldier and was decorated with medals for bravery. However,

Alpenhof, Adolph Hitler

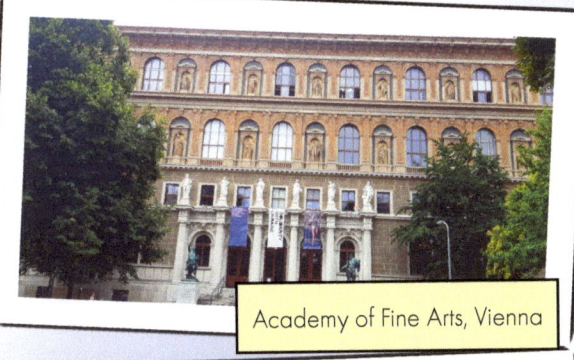

Academy of Fine Arts, Vienna

Painting of Karl Lueger at a ball

Georg Ritter von Schönerer

TIMELINE OF ADOLF HITLER'S LIFE

1889:   Adolf Hitler was born on April 20 in Braunau am Inn, Austria.

1907:   Hitler's mother passed away, and he moved to Vienna for a career in art, but was rejected by the Academy of Fine Arts.

1914:   World War I began, and Hitler joined the German Army, where he served as a soldier and was awarded the Iron Cross for bravery.

1918:   World War I ended, and Germany was defeated. Hitler was upset by the loss and blamed politicians and Jewish people for Germany's problems.

1923:   Hitler and his followers tried to overthrow the German government in an event called the Beer Hall Putsch. The attempt failed, and he was sent to prison.

1925:   While in prison, Hitler wrote *Mein Kampf*, *"My Struggle"*, a book about his ideas and plans for Germany.

1933:   Hitler became Chancellor of Germany. He quickly gained total power and turned Germany into a dictatorship.

1939:   World War II began when Germany, under Hitler's leadership, invaded Poland.

1941:   Hitler's army invaded the Soviet Union, and Germany was fighting against many powerful countries, including the United States, Britain, and the Soviet Union.

1945:   As World War II neared its end, Hitler hid in a bunker in Berlin. On April 30, he and his wife, Eva Braun, died in the bunker.

Adolph Hitler (far right, marked with an X in the Bavarian Army ~1914)

Troops arriving to support the Beer Hall Putsch

Hitler leaving a rally in Nuremberg in 1937

Hitler with girlfriend Eva Braun and dogs Blondi and Wulf

HITLER AS ARTIST

Adolf Hitler had dreams of becoming an artist, but his art career was marked by failure. After leaving school, he moved to Vienna in 1907 to follow his passion for painting. He applied to the Academy of Fine Arts Vienna but was rejected twice because his work was considered better suited for architecture than fine art. After his mother passed away the same year, Hitler struggled to support himself, often living in poverty. To make money, he painted and sold small watercolor pictures of Vienna's buildings and streets.

The Alter Hof in Munich, 1914

Some of his most recognized works include watercolor paintings like *The Alter Hof in Munich*, *Vienna State Opera House* and *Old Courtyard in Munich*, which show detailed architectural scenes. These paintings reveal his strong interest in buildings rather than people, as human figures in his art were often stiff and unrealistic. Despite creating hundreds of pieces, Hitler's artwork is mainly remembered today as a curiosity, reflecting the unfulfilled dreams of a man who later chose a path of destruction.

Die Karlskirche in Winter,
1912

Farewell to the Hunter, 1914

Neuschwanstein Castle,
1907

after Germany lost the war in 1918, Hitler was angry and bitter. The Treaty of Versailles signed on June 28, 1919 at the Paris Peace Conference had a lot of negative consequences on Germany for their role in the war. For example, Germany had to accept full blame for the war, paying full monetary reparations to other countries for the damage caused in the war, and other territorial and military losses. This treaty caused a lot of economic damage and shame to the country, and frustration to the people, which motivated individuals like Hitler looking to push for power.

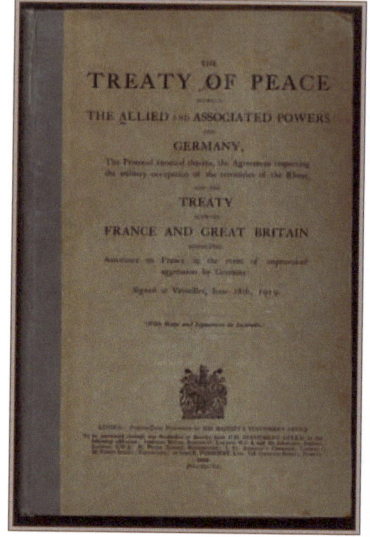

In 1919, Hitler joined a small political group called the German Workers' Party. He quickly became one of its leaders and helped turn it into the Nazi Party. Hitler was a powerful speaker, and he used speeches to spread his ideas about nationalism, anti-Semitism, and blaming Jews and Communists for Germany's problems.

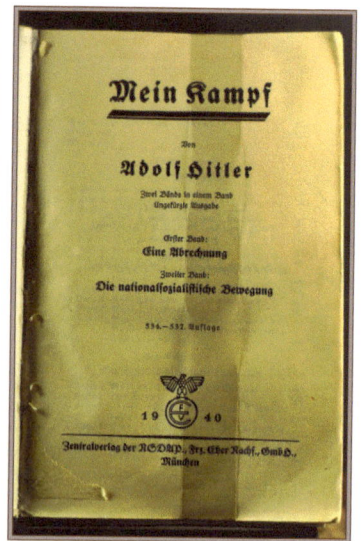

In 1923, he tried to take over the government in a failed coup attempt in Munich. He was arrested and sent to prison, where he began writing *Mein Kampf*, *"My Struggle"*, a book that explained his political ideas and plans for Germany. After his release in 1924, Hitler worked to gain support by promoting German nationalism and blaming Jews, communists, and international capitalism for Germany's problems. The Treaty of Versailles and

Germany's economic collapse increased Hitler's anger. He embraced the "stab-in-the-back" myth, the mistaken belief that the German Army did not lose the First World War on the battlefield, but was instead betrayed by communists, socialists and Jews pushing stereotypes and discrimination against these groups.

By 1933, the Nazi Party, led by Hitler, became the largest political party in Germany. That year, President Paul von Hindenburg appointed Hitler as Chancellor, the chief executive officer of Germany. Shortly afterward, the Enabling Act gave Hitler full power, turning Germany into a dictatorship under his control. Hitler's government focused on removing Jews from society and rebuilding Germany's power. His policies helped improve Germany's economy during his first years in power, but his plans were driven by hatred and a desire for war.

Hitler's first address as Chancellor to the German Parliament, the Reichstag, 1933

WHAT SPARKED ANTI-SEMITISM IN GERMANY?

Anti-Jewish feelings in Europe started long before Hitler and the Nazis. Jews were seen as different because they had their own religion and unique cultural traditions. A German historian named Klaus Fischer said the Jews were "an ancient cultured people." When Jews entered into Europe in large numbers during the Middle Ages, "they found themselves living among primitive Western people who were repelled by their superior intelligence and their clever business knowledge. There was mutual contempt and hate ... the two peoples were living alongside each other, but they were in different cultural stages." This caused both groups to dislike and mistrust each other.

A long time ago, most people lived in small towns or areas where everyone had the same religion and customs. Jews had their own religion (Judaism), holidays, and way of life, which were different from the majority. People often fear or don't trust what they don't understand, and that fear can lead to unfair treatment. When bad things happened, such as plagues, wars, or economic problems, people sometimes blamed Jews even though they had nothing to do with it. This is called being a scapegoat — being blamed for problems caused by something or someone else. Jews were sometimes successful in business, especially since some jobs were closed to them and they had to find other ways to make money. This success led to jealousy.

Also, false stories (called myths) were made up about Jews, such as saying they were greedy or evil, which wasn't true. In some places, people blamed Jews for things that went wrong, especially in Christian countries. For example, during the Middle Ages, some Christians blamed Jews for the death of Jesus, even though Jesus himself was Jewish. This caused anger and hatred. In many countries, laws were made that treated Jews unfairly. They were forced to live in certain areas (like ghettos), wear special clothes, or banned from owning land. This made them more separated from others, which continued the cycle of discrimination. These differences—religion, culture, and suspicion of outsiders—created a lot of tension. Over time, this tension led to violence. When Hitler rose to power, he used this long history of hate to blame the Jews for Germany's problems.

After Germany's defeat in World War I, the Treaty of Versailles, and the subsequent economic collapse, Jews were falsely blamed for Germany's loss and financial crises. When Hitler and the Nazis took control, they used these false stories to make people hate Jews even more. They passed laws and used propaganda to blame and abuse the Jewish people, which led to the Holocaust.

Concentration camp uniform with a yellow star labeled Jew

German tanks in Finland

US Soldiers in Germany

Hitler with Benito Mussolini, leader of Italy

Soviet Army at the Battle of Stalingrad

Hitler wanted to expand Germany's territory to create more "living space" (*Lebensraum*) for its people, especially in Eastern Europe. His aggressive actions led to World War II, starting with the invasion of Poland on September 1, 1939. Britain and France declared war on Germany shortly after. Hitler's forces quickly took over much of Europe, including Poland, Norway, Denmark, Netherlands, Belgium, Luxembourg, France, Greece, Yugoslavia, Austria, and Italy. Italy began as an ally of Germany; however, after Italy surrendered to United States and British forces, Germany marched in and seized Rome.

In 1941, he invaded the Soviet Union. Later that year, he declared war on the United States, bringing them into the conflict.

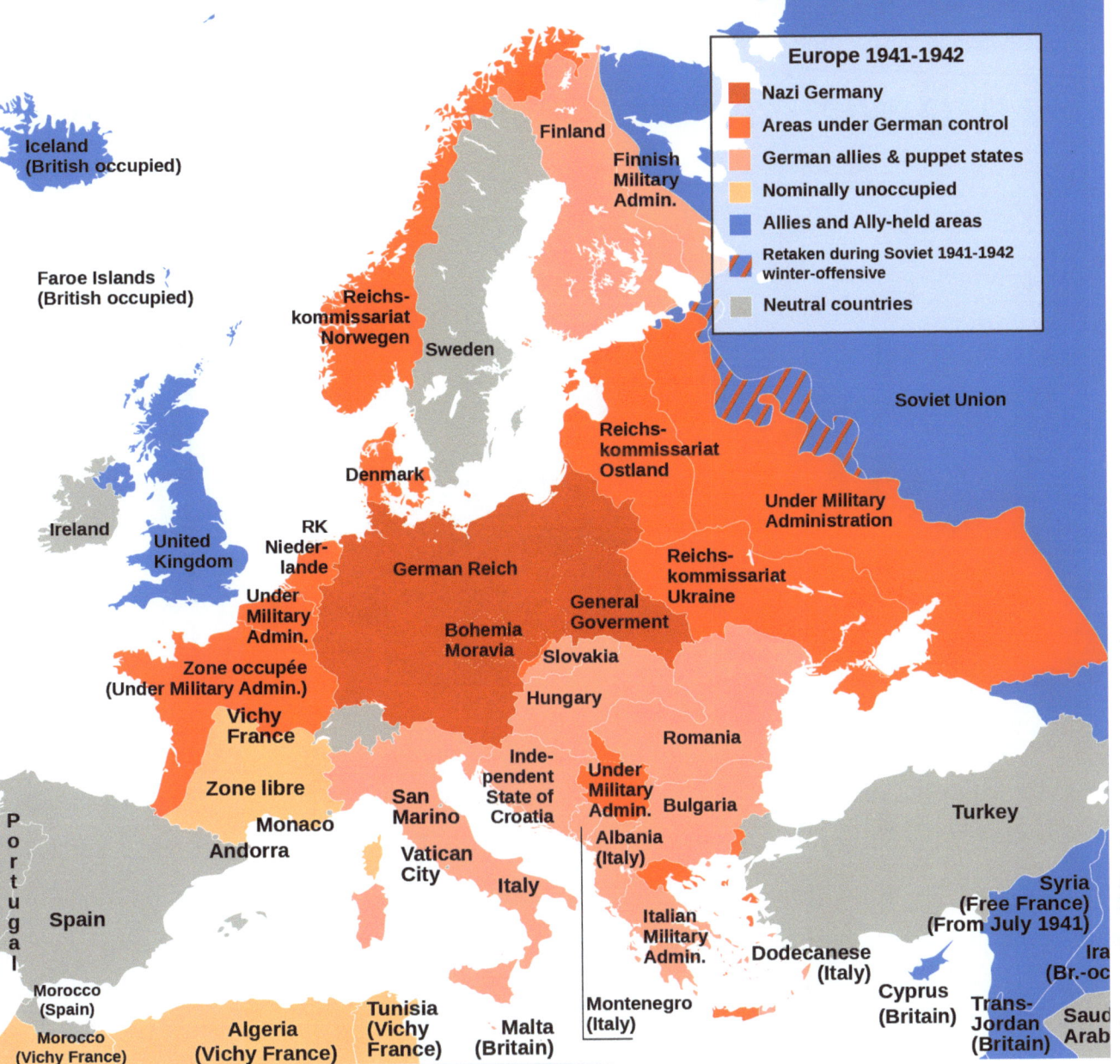

Europe 1941-1942

- Nazi Germany
- Areas under German control
- German allies & puppet states
- Nominally unoccupied
- Allies and Ally-held areas
- Retaken during Soviet 1941-1942 winter-offensive
- Neutral countries

Iceland
(British occupied)

Faroe Islands
(British occupied)

Finland

Finnish
Military
Admin.

Reichs-
kommissariat
Norwegen

Sweden

Soviet Union

Reichs-
kommissariat
Ostland

Denmark

Under Military
Administration

Ireland

United
Kingdom

RK
Nieder-
lande

German Reich

Reichs-
kommissariat
Ukraine

Under
Military
Admin.

Bohemia
Moravia

General
Goverment

Zone occupée
(Under Military Admin.)

Slovakia

Vichy
France

Hungary

Romania

Zone libre

Inde-
pendent
State of
Croatia

Under
Military
Admin.

Bulgaria

Turkey

Monaco

San
Marino

Andorra

Albania
(Italy)

Vatican
City

Portugal

Italy

Spain

Italian
Military
Admin.

Dodecanese
(Italy)

Syria
(Free France)
(From July 1941)

Morocco
(Spain)

Montenegro
(Italy)

Cyprus
(Britain)

Ira
(Br.-oc

Morocco
(Vichy France)

Algeria
(Vichy France)

Tunisia
(Vichy
France)

Malta
(Britain)

Trans-
Jordan
(Britain)

Saud
Arab

However, Germany began to lose as the Soviet Union pushed back and the U.S. helped the Allies, which included many nations, including the "Big 4" of the US, the UK, the Soviet Union, and China.

The last days of Adolf Hitler are surrounded by mystery and debate. In April 1945, as World War II was ending, Hitler hid in a bunker in Berlin while the city was being attacked by Soviet forces. On

AUSCHWITZ: THE WORST CONCENTRATION CAMP?

Gates of Auschwitz, text reading
"Work Sets You Free"

Auschwitz was a large concentration camp (a prison camp where a group is confined) and extermination camp (a death camp or a place people are killed) camp built by the Nazis during World War II in occupied Poland. It became a central part of the Holocaust, where millions of Jews, along with Romani people, political prisoners, and others, were imprisoned, forced into labor, or killed.

The camp complex included Auschwitz I, the main camp; Auschwitz II - Birkenau, a death camp with gas chambers; and Auschwitz III - Monowitz, a labor camp. Conditions were inhumane, with overcrowding, starvation, and brutal treatment. including limited food, dirty conditions, and common

Entrance to
Auschwitz-Birkeneau II

beatings and violence. For example, the gold teeth of victims were sometimes even ripped out while the people were still alive and what little food was available would also be stolen by rats.

Today, Auschwitz is a symbol of the horrors of the Holocaust and a memorial to its victims.

Aerial Photo of Auschwitz, 1944

Estimates of prisoners and victims at the Auschwitz complex

- Jews: (1,095,000, 960,000 killed)
- Poles: (140,000-150,000 deported, 74,000 killed)
- Roma: (23,000 deported, 21,000 died)
- Soviet POWs: (15,000 deported and killed)
- Other nationalities (25,000 deported, 10,000-15,000 killed)

Selection of prisoners on the ramp at Auschwitz

Prisoner barracks

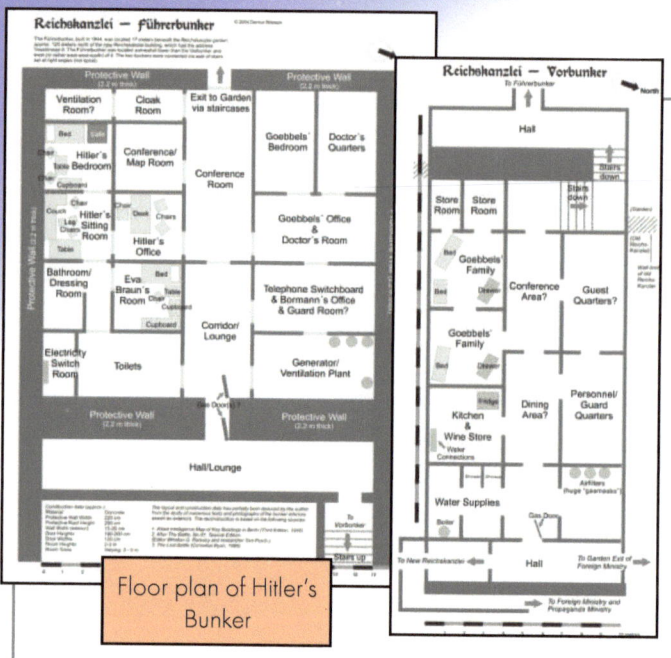

Floor plan of Hitler's Bunker

April 30, he and his wife, Eva Braun, were said to have died, and their bodies were burned.

However, some people have questioned this story, wondering if he might have escaped. Over the years, rumors spread about Hitler fleeing to places like South America, but most historians who studied the life of Hitler believe he died in the bunker. His final days remain a topic of interest and speculation. But what is known is that Adolf Hitler is seen as one of history's most monstrous figures.

Under Hitler's leadership, the Nazis were responsible for the deaths of at least

Site of Hitler's Führerbunker

6 million Jewish people in the Holocaust. Millions of others, including prisoners of war, people with disabilities, and political opponents, were also murdered. In total, Hitler's actions and World War II caused the deaths of over 70 million people. This makes it the deadliest conflict in human history. But what if Hitler had been stopped or had never risen to power? This is a question that has been asked by historians for decades!

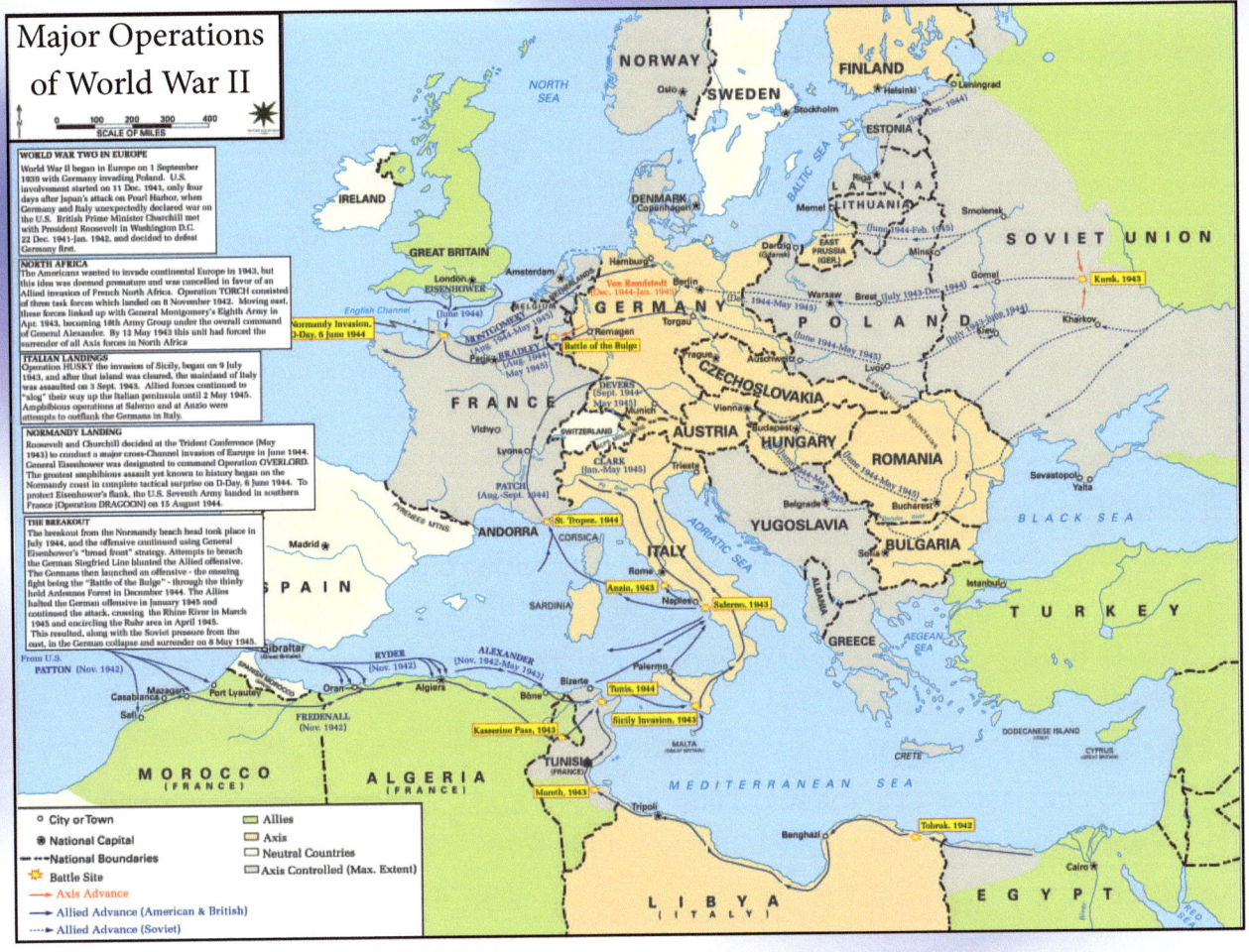

LEARN MORE

World War Two: An overview from BBC Bitesize: www.bbc.co.uk/bitesize/articles/z6vff82#zb7jjsg

"Is this what the world would look like if Hitler never existed?" from Grunge: www.grunge.com/1613620/is-this-what-world-would-look-like-if-hitler-never-existed/

"Adolf Hiter: Rise to power, impact & death." from History.com: www.history.com/articles/adolf-hitler.

"Adolf Hitler" on Wikipedia: https://en.wikipedia.org/wiki/Adolf_Hitler.

HITLER IN FILM AND MEDIA

Movies about Adolf Hitler range from serious historical dramas and documentaries to satire and speculative films. These films explore his life, ideology, and impact on history, often sparking debate due to their subject matter. Here's a list of some of the most important films about Hitler:

Historical Dramas

Downfall, Der Untergang (2004)
Director: Oliver Hirschbiegel
Plot: Chronicles Hitler's final days in his Berlin bunker during the Battle of Berlin in 1945. Based on eyewitness accounts, it provides a powerful and humanizing (yet unsympathetic) portrayal of his demise.
Note: Bruno Ganz received critical praise for his complex acting as Hitler.
Hitler: The Rise of Evil (2003)
Director: Christian Duguay
Plot: A miniseries dramatizing Hitler's early years and his rise to power, from his childhood through to becoming Chancellor of Germany.
Note: Robert Carlyle stars as Hitler, focusing on the personal and political dynamics that shaped his ascent.
The Bunker (1981)
Director: George Schaefer
Plot: Another depiction of Hitler's final days in the bunker, based on James P. O'Donnell's book.
Note: Anthony Hopkins delivers an interesting performance as Hitler.

Documentaries

Triumph of the Will, Triumph des Willens (1935)
Director: Leni Riefenstahl
Plot: A film glorifying Hitler and the Nazi Party during the 1934 Nuremberg Rally.
Note: Although controversial, it's recognized as an excellent example of a propaganda film, one that presents a specific opinion. The film offers insight into how Hitler's image was crafted.
The Hitler Chronicles, Die Hitler-Chronik (2018)

Director: Hermann Pölking

Plot: A four-part documentary using rare archival footage and Hitler's own writings to chronicle his life.

Note: An extensive exploration of Hitler's personal and political journey.

Satirical and Speculative Films

The Great Dictator (1940)

Director: Charlie Chaplin

Plot: A satirical comedy about a Jewish barber who looks like a fictional dictator, "Adenoid Hynkel," a parody of Hitler.

Note: Chaplin's critique of fascism and his iconic closing speech about compassion and democracy.

Look Who's Back, Er ist wieder da (2015)

Director: David Wnendt

Plot: A satirical film imagining Hitler waking up in modern-day Germany and becoming a media sensation.

Note: Examines contemporary attitudes toward Hitler and far-right ideologies through dark humor.

Jojo Rabbit (2019)

Director: Taika Waititi

Plot: A comedic drama about a young boy in Nazi Germany whose imaginary friend is a silly, strange version of Hitler.

Note: Taika Waititi's humorous yet poignant critique of blind nationalism.

Other Notable Films

Mein Kampf (2010)

Director: Urs Odermatt

Plot: A dark comedy-drama imagining Hitler's time in Vienna and his failed attempts to gain admission to art school.

Note: Explores the seeds of his ideology through speculative fiction.

Max (2002)

Director: Menno Meyjes

Plot: A fictional account of Hitler's life as a struggling artist in post-World War I Germany, focusing on his relationship with a Jewish art dealer.

Note: Examines the intersection of art, politics, and ideology.

What If Hitler Had Been Stopped?

If Hitler had been stopped early, the chain of events leading to World War II might have been avoided or delayed. Without his aggressive expansionist policies and militarization, Europe may have been more stable, as it was already struggling with economic challenges and the consequences of WWI.

However, even without Hitler, Germany's economic struggles and resentment from the Treaty of Versailles might have given rise to another authoritarian figure. Hitler was not the only cause of Germany's issues, but rather a product of them.

Stopping Hitler could have prevented the Holocaust, but anti-Semitism and persecution of Jews in Europe might have persisted in other forms. Anti-Semitism was and has been present in many forms around the world. Would other world leaders carry out anti-semitic policies like Hitler?

WHY DOES IT MATTER

Adolf Hitler was one of the most important and tragic figures in history because of the impact he had on the world. As the leader of Nazi Germany during World War II, he started a war that caused massive destruction and the deaths of millions of people. Hitler is also remembered for the Holocaust, during which millions of Jewish people and other groups were murdered in one of history's worst genocides.

His actions changed the course of the 20th century, leading to the end of World War II and shaping how countries work together today to prevent such events from happening again. Hitler's story is a reminder of the dangers of hatred and unchecked power. The Nazis and their anti-Semitism legacy sadly lives on in neo-Nazis which still exist today.

SURPRISING FACTS

Hitler Wanted to Be an Artist

He dreamed of becoming a painter and applied twice to the Academy of Fine Arts Vienna, but was rejected both times.

He Was a Vegetarian

Later in life, Hitler followed a mostly vegetarian diet and even banned animal cruelty in Nazi Germany, which led to some of the earliest animal welfare laws in the world.

He Loved Disney Movies

Hitler was said to have admired Disney films, especially *Snow White and the Seven Dwarfs*. He even made sketches of Disney characters.

He Was a Dog Lover

Hitler had a strong affection for dogs, especially his German Shepherd, Blondi. He was known to spend lots of time training and caring for his pets.

He Was Claustrophobic

Hitler disliked enclosed spaces and had elevators modified to ensure he felt comfortable using them.

Hitler Avoided Coffee and Alcohol

He didn't drink alcohol most of his life and preferred herbal tea over coffee.

He Designed the Volkswagen Beetle

Hitler worked with engineer Ferdinand Porsche to create the concept for the Volkswagen Beetle, aiming to provide an affordable car for German families.

He Was Time Magazine's Person of the Year in 1938

Time Magazine named Hitler "Man of the Year" in 1938 for his impact on global politics. This was not an honor but a recognition of his significant (and controversial) influence.

GLOSSARY

rhetoric (n) - effective language

ghetto (n) - part of a city, often a poor area, where people of a particular race or religion live

decorated (adj) - (here) awarded

anti-Semitism (n) - prejudice and racist discrimination against Jewish people

nationalism (n) - placing one's own country above all others

dictatorship (n) - a one-party rule with a single leader at the top

genocide (adj) - the murder of a large population of people

speculation (n) - the act or process of thinking, wondering, or guessing about something

DISCUSSION QUESTIONS

1. What do you know about concentration camps? What did you learn from this reading?

2. What events influenced Hitler's outlook and policies? What led him to become Germany's leader and his views of anti-semitism and starting World War II?

3. Do you think you could stop Hitler from becoming the leader of Germany? How could you influence his beliefs? For example, would you try to talk to Hitler, or kill him?

4. It is claimed by some that Hitler faked his own death. Do you think that's possible? Why or why not?

5. Who is another leader in history with an evil reputation?

6. Read the following quote from Mein Kampf. What do you think it means?

    "Those who want to live, let them fight, and those who do not want to fight in this world of eternal struggle do not deserve to live."

PROJECTS

1. Find one source that supports the conspiracy theory that Hitler survived World War II and one that claims he didn't. Compare the biases in each one. Which is more believable?

2. Research about Hitler: Write about 1 page and answer one or both questions below

   • What were his most evil achievements?

   • How did Hitler's rule in Germany affect or change world history?

3. What if Hitler had lived and Germany had won World War II? Research at least one theory or idea on what he might have done.

4. Rank from likely to unlikely the theories as presented in the chapter on what would have happened if Hitler was stopped.

5. Write an essay: Are monsters like Hitler born or made? How did his life contribute to his actions as leader of Germany, the Holocaust, and WWII?

6. Jewish people have faced discrimination throughout history. Research one example and write a paragraph describing the time, locations, how Jewish people faced discrimination, and what the results were.

7. Write a story! Write about a page. Here are some questions to consider as you write:

   • Can you stop Hitler?

   • How can you stop him

REFERENCES

Bullock, Alan Louis Charles. *Hitler: A Study in Tyranny*. Harmondsworth: Penguin, 1962.

Evans, Richard J. *The Coming of the Third Reich*. London: Penguin, 2003.

Evans, Richard J. *The Third Reich in Power*. New York: Penguin Books, 2006.

Ferguson, Niall. *Virtual History: Alternatives and Counterfactuals*. Basic Books, 1997.

Hamann, Brigitte, and Henry J. Cohn. *Hitler's Vienna: A Dictator's Apprenticeship*. New York: Oxford University Press, 1999.

Hiller, N. "Treaty of Versailles." The Canadian Encyclopedia, March 4, 2015. https://thecanadianencyclopedia.ca/en/article/treaty-of-versailles.

Hitler, Adolf, and E. T. S. Dugdale. *My Battle*. Boston: Houghton Mifflin, 2001.

Kershaw, Ian. *Hitler: A Biography*. New York: W.W. Norton & Company, 2008.

Kershaw, Ian. *The "Hitler Myth": Image and Reality in the Third Reich*. Oxford: Oxford University Press, 1987.

Mommsen, Hans, and Elborg Forster. *Rise and Fall of Weimar Democracy*. Chapel Hill: The University of North Carolina Press, 1996.

Nakatani, Mina. "Is This What the World Would Look Like If Hitler Never Existed?" Grunge, July 7, 2024. https://www.grunge.com/1613620/is-this-what-world-would-look-like-if-hitler-never-existed.

Payne, Stanley G. *A History of Fascism 1914-1945*. Abingdon-on-Thames: Routledge, 1996.

Shirer, William L. *The Rise and Fall of the Third Reich: A History of Nazi Germany*. New York: Simon and Schuster, 1960.

Timothy, Snyder. *Bloodlands: Europe between Hitler and Stalin*. New York: Basic Books, 2010.

United States Holocaust Museum. "Antisemitism in History: Nazi Antisemitism." United States Holocaust Memorial Museum, n.d. https://encyclopedia.ushmm.org/content/en/article/antisemitism-in-history-nazi-antisemitism.

Weber, Thomas. *Hitler's First War: Adolf Hitler, the Men of the List Regiment, and the First World War*. Oxford: Oxford University Press, 2010. .

ISBN: 978-1-956159-63-9 (print)

29 Milo Dr. Branford, CT 06405 USA
info@alphabetpublishingbooks.com
www.AlphabetPublishingBooks.com

Discounts on class sets and bulk orders available upon inquiry.

Cover and Interior Design by Walton Burns

Country of Manufacture Specified on Last Page

First Printing 2025

Images

cover left Wikimedia/Unknown, PD • cover top right Wikimedia/Xiquinho Silva, CC by-SA 2.0 • cover bottom right Wikimedia/Wikinst, CC by-SA 3.0 • pg. i Wikimedia/RsVe, modified by Walton Burns, CC 0 • pg. ii top Wikimedia/Xiquinho Silva, CC by-SA 2.0 • pg. ii middle Wikimedia/Unknown, PD • pg. ii bottom Wikimedia/Unknown / Adolph Hitler, PD • pg. 6 left Wikimedia/Josef Reinegger, PD • pg. 6 center Wikimedia/Josef Franz Kilnger, PD • pg. 6 right Wikimedia/Unknown, PD • pg. 7 top Wikimedia/Unknown, PD • pg. 7 top middle Wikimedia/Armineaghayan, CC by-SA 4.0 • pg. 7 bottom middle Wikimedia/Wilhem Gausse, PD • pg. 7 bottom Wikimedia/Unknown, PD • pg. 9 top Wikimedia/NARA, PD • pg. 9 top middle National Archives/Unknown, PD • pg. 9 bottom middle Wikimedia/Unknown, PD • pg. 9 bottom Wikimedia/Unknown, PD • pg. 10 Wikimedia/Unknown, PD • pg. 11 top Wikimedia/Unknown, PD • pg. 11 middle Wikimedia/Unknown, PD • pg. 11 bottom Wikimedia/Unknown, PD • pg. 12 top Wikimedia/Unknown, PD • pg. 12 bottom Wikimedia/Eher Verlag, PD • pg. 13 National Archives/Unknown, PD • pg. 15 Wikimedia/Istvan Takacs, CC by-SA 3.0 • pg. 16 top Wikimedia/Finnish Military, PD • pg. 16 top middle Wikimedia/PFC J. F. Musae, PD • pg. 16 bottom middle Wikimedia/Eva Braun, PD • pg. 16 bottom Wikimedia/Semyon Vladimirovich, CC by-SA 3.0 • pg. 17 Wikimedia (colors modified)/Goran tek-en, CC by-SA 4.0 • pg. 18 top Wikimedia/Xiquinho Silva, CC by-SA 2.0 • pg. 18 bottom Wikimedia/Jacob M. Ramos, CC by-SA 2.0 • pg. 19 top Wikimedia/South Africa Air Force, PD • pg. 19 middle Wikimedia/Walter Bernhard, PD • pg. 19 bottom Wikimedia/China Crisis, CC by-SA 3.0 • pg. 20 top left and top right Wikimedia/Dna-Dennis, CC by-SA 3.0 • pg. 20 bottom Wikimedia/Richard Mortel, CC by-SA 2.0 • pg. 21 Wikimedia/US Military Academy, PD • pg. 22 Depositphotos/stillfix, licensed • pg. 28 Wikimedia/Paul Wolf, PD

www.ingramcontent.com/pod-product-compliance
Lightning Source LLC
Chambersburg PA
CBHW041441120626

46547CB00002B/302